The Little Voodoo Kit

revenge therapy for the over-stressed

Published in Great Britain in 1997 by

Michael O'Mara Books Limited
9 Lion Yard
Tremadoc Road
London SW4 7NQ

A CIP catalogue record for this book is available from the British Library

1 3 5 7 9 10 8 6 4 2

ISBN 1-85479-324-1

Designed by Carruthers Elliott Fine

Illustrations by Fran Stevens

Special thanks to Mike Janulewicz, Katie Preston and Cameron Carruthers.

Printed and bound in Hong Kong through Printlink International Co

Warning

This book, doll and pins is intended as a humorous item. It is not a child's toy and is only
intended for use by responsible adults and is not intended for use by children. It does not
comply with Toy Safety Legislation. The publisher, copyright holder and the author shall
not be liable individually or severally for any damage that may be caused or sustained
as a result of conducting any of the activities or following any of the instructions
contained in this book or by using the doll and pins included in The Little Voodoo Kit.

THE LITTLE
Voodoo
KIT

Dr J.P. Poupette

Michael O'Mara Books Limited

About the Author

Dr Jean-Paul Poupette is Professor of Stress Research at Idongotu University, the Celebeles. The only son of a missionary he lived throughout the South Pacific Islands and the Caribbean during his early years, learning the folk beliefs of many different peoples, before taking a degree in Comparative Religion at the Missionary College, Santa Sardinia.

His legendary treatise on Acupuncture, Voodoo Pins and Popular Music in the Modern World elegantly proved the link between Tao philosophy, reggae music and such classic hits of the 1960s as Needles and Pins by the Searchers and the unforgettable Living Doll by British rocker Cliff Richard.

Dr Poupette's most recent research shows that the ultimate solution to stress, whatever its cause, is revenge therapy. This therapy has been practised worldwide for thousands of years and has been the basis for a peaceful co-existence between, and within, many societies. The research has culminated in this prestigious book, which offers practical help to today's stressed individuals. Dr Poupette also runs 'de-stress' seminars and workshops for high-flying business executives.

Contents

Introduction

Dolls and human likenesses of all kinds have played an important and positive role in societies from Ancient Egypt, through the rise and fall of the Empires of Greece and Rome, to the present day. They have been used as charms to weave magical spells, amulets to protect the bearer from ill-luck and talismans to bring good fortune. They have been offered to the Gods to cure all kinds of illness and, in their ultimate expression, have become the great statues that the rich, powerful and famous have erected to buy their immortality.

It is sad that the concept of the doll as powerful protector has been distorted in low-budget horror films and second-rate novels. Extensive research has proved that the correct use of dolls and other human symbols can bring peace and tranquillity to the practitioner's life. Although it is often referred to as revenge therapy, **this practice is not about causing harm to other people, but is designed to release anger and stress in the user.** By ritualising anger and stress through revenge therapy, the feelings are dissipated, and there is no need for open conflict.

Research shows that stress is one of the greatest killers today. Stress causes depression, increases the likelihood of heart problems and reduces the body's ability to recover from illnesses. My team at Idongotu University has devised experiments that prove the effectiveness of revenge therapy: it reduces blood pressure, heart rate, cholesterol levels and encourages the production of endorphins in the brain, which bring feelings of well-being. In just three weeks, stressed-out students have been turned from hair-tearers to gift-bearers, from insomniacs to sleepers, from pit bulls to labradors.

In the Idongotu stress laboratory, volunteers are wired up to EEG, ECG, REM, EGG, CATS, TOMS and muscle synergetic monitors and exposed to a simulated stress situation using the latest interactive multimedia technology. As **stress triggers**, such as road rage, bank managers' smugness, estate agents' patronisation, revenue collectors' intransigence and irritating TV 'personalities', are brought to life, the subject is monitored for every physiological change to calibrate their normal reaction.

On day two, the **revenge therapy doll** and strategies are introduced into the situations and are shown to have an immediate effect. With careful training, and by following my master course, the volunteer can within three weeks **control all anger and dramatically reduce stress levels**. The chart below provides a fascinating summary of the research team's work. Some students further claim that their doll can cure baldness, eliminate spots and other skin eruptions and helps make them irresistible to the opposite sex. You must make your own judgements but, remember, to those who walk with the doll all things can be possible.

Stress Readings: Idongotu University Stress Research Project 1994–6

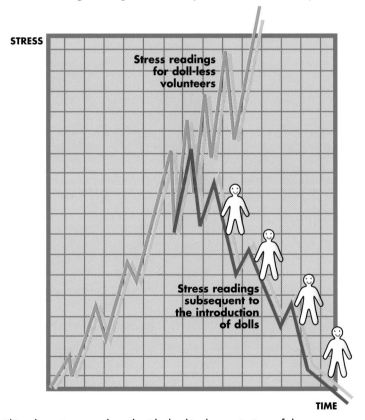

This chart is reproduced with the kind permission of the stress research team at Idongotu University. Particular thanks go to the volunteers who participated in the experiments. Readers will be relieved to know that the doll-less control group recovered after intensive revenge therapy, kindly provided free of charge by the research team.

DOLL POWER

'The doll with many pinholes is the doll whose master sleeps peacefully at night and greets every day with a smile.'

From *The Way of the Doll*

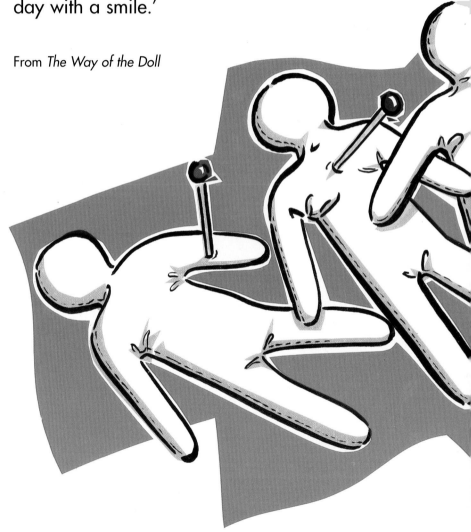

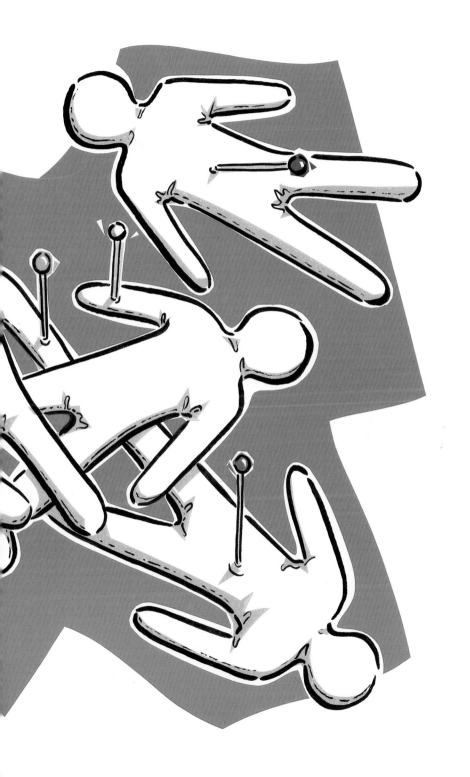

You and Your Doll

For successful stress relief there are two important principles – know your doll and know your pins. And, since practice makes perfect, the dedicated revenge therapy student should study for at least ten minutes each day. First, it is essential to bond with your doll both physically and emotionally. Using the technique known as *moturo*, massage your doll between thumb and forefinger. **Always keep your thumb on the front of the doll as you learn its shape and texture.** During moturo you should relax and make your mind go blank until a name comes into your thoughts. This is the name that will belong to the doll's spirit forever. This name is known as the *muramba*, and must never be revealed to anyone else.

The diagram opposite illustrates the key areas, or segments, of your doll. The beginner can gain immediate relief by inserting pins into any segment, but the more sophisticated student will want to choose the appropriate segment with thought and care. Taking time over such subtle decisions are a major factor in achieving **significant, long-term stress relief**.

All students should note that the doll should be placed face up on a soft surface before pin insertion begins. A powerful therapy is in play and I can take no responsibility for students who do not obey this simple rule.

Many students dedicate a special cushion or pillow to this purpose. Indeed new research may show that the doll who reclines happily on its own pillow will be a more powerful and effective friend to you. Never risk damaging your pins or yourself by random, uncontrolled pin insertion. For emergency use we recommend using a rolled up sweater or jacket.

Some beginners are concerned to know which is the front and which the back of their doll. Be reassured that the knowledge will come as you get to **know your doll more intimately**.

Serious doll students and researchers are locked in a debate over the significance of the relative importance of the right and left side of the doll. The beginner need not concern themselves with this debate but might like to take into account that left-handed disciples have reported feeling more benefit using the left-hand side of the doll. No such data has been recorded on right-handed users.

Significant Segments

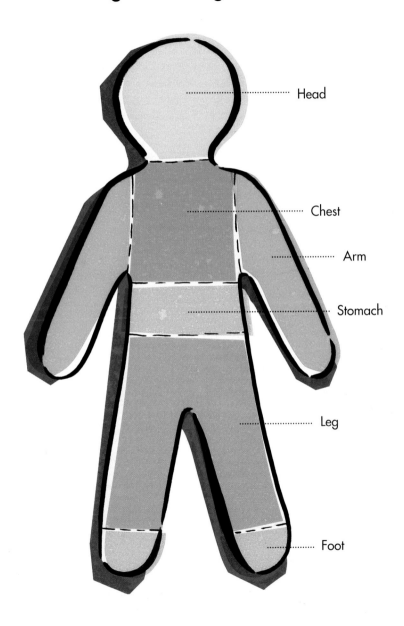

Head

Chest

Arm

Stomach

Leg

Foot

Getting the Point

Only when you feel comfortable with your doll should you begin practising with the pins, developing the techniques that relieve stress or satisfy an **acute desire for revenge**. There is a correct order in which these techniques should be learned and a special significance to the colour of the pins. Only move on to the next lesson when you have mastered the previous one.

With all of these insertion techniques the pin should go into the doll. **The doll should never be pulled on to the pin.** Remember to position your doll on a soft surface before you begin. The pin must be held between index finger and thumb of the right hand. Left-handers are warned that using the left hand may reduce the power of insertion.

Once you have mastered all of these lessons, you will have achieved the status of **Bigandra** (Master). At Idongotu University stress seminars, students dress their dolls in sashes of the appropriate colour to indicate the level that they have achieved. A red sash carries much status.

One: *baranda* (slow insertion)

Always use the white pin. Insert it as slowly as you can. It should then be left in the doll for the same amount of time as it took to insert, and withdrawn at the same speed. Counting 'one, two, three…' very slowly helps to establish a good rhythm. Practise each move ten times.

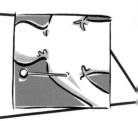

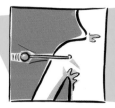

Two: *cabara* (jabbing motion)

Use the yellow pin, building up the speed of insertion as you practise. Try to keep the pin at right angles to the doll's body. This technique is a favourite with beginners, but lacks subtlety.

Three: *darana* (slow insertion at a 45° angle)

Use the green pin. The *darana* is always used slowly as the correct angle is the important element. Practise as for **baranda.**

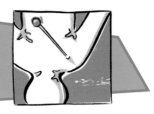

Four: *nandra* (slow insertion of the pin with a twist)

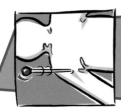

Use the blue pin. Slowly insert the pin at a right angle and then twist slowly clockwise for as long as necessary to feel relaxed. Repeat five times for serious stress situations.

Five: *panandra* (slow insertion at acute angle with twist)

Use the pink pin. This differs from **nandra** in the fact that the pin is twisted as it is inserted. This is a very powerful technique to be reserved for seriously stressful situations.

Six: *totandranba* (combined baranda and cabara)

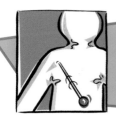

Use the red pin. This technique uses two short jabs, followed by one slow insertion. This is repeated until all frustration and tension has gone. Only to be used in situations of severe stress.

Doll Strategies

Doll revenge therapy is not only about knowing the techniques of pinning, but also about training your mind and understanding the significant energy points on the doll's body. Refer back to the diagram on page 11 if necessary.

Energy Points

The pins should be inserted into appropriate parts, or segments, of the doll depending on the cause of your frustration and stress.

Head For relieving stress caused by people who have spoken against you.

Chest For relief of the stress caused by people who have put obstacles in your way.

Stomach For relief of the stress caused by people who have made you look bad in front of others

Arms For relief of the stress caused by people whose stupidity and incompetence has made your life difficult.

Legs For relief of the stress caused by people who have held up your progress – whether in your career or in your car.

Never forget that the object of revenge therapy is not to harm someone who has slighted you. The idea is to relieve YOU of the stress that the incident has caused by helping you to diminish the power of the perpetrator.

Training the mind should begin while practising the pinning techniques. First you must imagine the doll has transmuted into the person on whom you seek revenge and then let your mind fill with the wrong that they have done. Choose the **correct pinning technique and energy point** and keep working until the bad thoughts dissipate and finally disappear altogether.

You are now in a state that the Masters call *vallhandra* and your mind, if fully trained, will flood with the feelings of revenge satisfactorily completed. You will be able to greet the person who has so distressed you with a happy smile showing their behaviour cannot touch the inner you – surely the best revenge of all.

Whole-doll Techniques

Severe long-term frustration may need more drastic measures, which involve the loss or destruction of the doll. Household pets have plenty of potential. **Stuff the doll with catnip**, a herb that will send even the most docile cat into a frenzy, and watch it savaged and pawed around the room.

Allowing your doll to disappear from sight can help to draw severe stress out of you. Letting the doll float away down a river is very soothing – imagine it reaching an oil slick in the sea in a few days' time. **Posting the doll to some distant and unpleasant place or leaving it on a train bound to Alaska can exorcise most of your worst feelings.**

The art of these techniques is to make the demise of the doll appropriate to your situation. Take time to decide on a course of action – thinking about revenge therapy can be therapeutic in itself.

Make Your Own Doll

Revenge therapy students will need a ready supply of dolls. Making your own is quite simple and indeed is a highly therapeutic activity in its own right. Stuffing a new doll can be made into a simple ceremony, accompanied by the judicious consumption of alcohol. Brandy is highly recommended.

You will need

Brown paper

Pencil

Scissors

Cotton fabric (approx 24cm x 20cm)

Pins

Needle and thread

Stuffing material (see page 18 for suggestions)

1. Copy or trace the pattern opposite on to a piece of brown paper. Cut out the shape to make a template. Remember that the cutting line is outside the sewing line as you need to allow 1cm for the seam.

2. Fold the fabric in half, pin on the template, and cut out two identical doll shapes. Pin together along the sewing line and stitch the seams, leaving a 3cm gap along the thigh.

3. Turn the doll inside out so that the seams are hidden. Stuff with your chosen material and sew up the gap.

Detailed Decoration

If you wish, and it can be helpful in some stressful situations, to disguise your doll as a harmless children's toy or souvenir, you can add hair and a face. The features can be drawn on with a felt-tip pen or embroidered. A belly button adds authenticity.

Doll Pattern

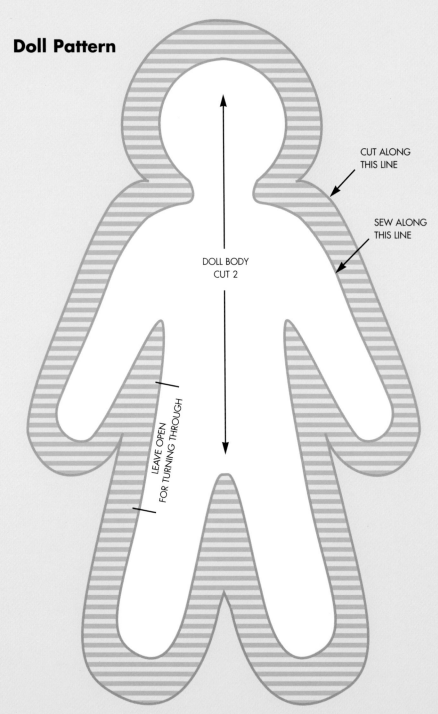

CUT ALONG
THIS LINE

SEW ALONG
THIS LINE

DOLL BODY
CUT 2

LEAVE OPEN
FOR TURNING THROUGH

Tailor-made Magic

Y ou are probably just beginning to understand the subtlety and range of the power of your doll. The power does not lie only in the manipulation of pins. If you are prepared to make your own doll (see page 16) you can tailor it to match your specific requirements, whether you want to win the lottery, get your own back on enemies, or make the local stud or super-babe swoon with desire for you.

Forget aromatherapy, revenge therapy is much more useful when it comes to relieving you of your worries, whether they are money, health, work or love related. Of course, it doesn't hurt to borrow a few elements of aromatherapy to enhance the development and performance of your doll skills. Filling your revenge therapy doll with **aromatic herbs can strengthen the desired effect** when you are practising your magic, provided you match the stuffing to the occasion.

The information on the opposite page will give you guidance on which herbs will best serve your purpose. Fresh herbs are, of course, the most effective but dried herbs are worth trying. Stuff the doll, insert the herbs and then sew up the opening.

Reluctant sewers can unpick the seams of their first or 'given' doll and insert herbs but this practice really cannot be recommended. It has been known to upset a doll severely with **potentially disastrous results**. If you really can't make your own doll it is best to commission one under the guise of having a dear little dolly made for a favourite niece, or nephew.

All of the herbs pictured opposite are also available as **essential oils**. They can be used in this form to anoint the head of your doll prior to pin insertion when you are particularly stressed. Breathe deeply and insert the pin using the darana technique (see page 13) to gain the full benefit.

Wealth
comfrey
lemon verbena
marjoram
thyme

Love
lavender
lovage
orange blossom
rose petals

Luck
basil
chamomile
parsley
rosemary

**Defeating
Enemies**
catnip
poppy seed
rue
wormwood

**Success
in Projects**
bay leaves
hops
peppermint

Health
marigold
sage
thyme

Case Studies

The results achieved with voodoo dolls and revenge therapy are certainly remarkable. Here, three individuals, from very different walks of life, give testimony to how their lives were changed forever after discovering 'doll power'.

Brian Honey, Entrepreneur and Electronics Magnate

I used to sell radios and clocks on a market stall and was doing quite well, actually. Certainly enough to take a holiday to Indonesia to get away from it all. It was there that I discovered the power of the doll. It seemed daft at first – me, streetwise and tough, playing with a doll!

But incredibly it seemed to work. I started to see clearly and realised that the future was in computers and other electronic gadgets. I was a millionaire within three years and even now I don't make a business decision without using my doll first. It sits on my desk all the time. I am developing a web site where doll students can seek information. I would recommend using dolls to anyone who wants to be rich and famous.

See you on the Internet, Brian

Princess Irene

I was a quiet girl whose only interest was sewing and embroidery when I met my future husband. He was very interested in alternative things – you know medicines and other philosophies. Well, there I was making some doll's clothes for my local charity shop when it all sort of happened. It was definitely his doll that brought us together – it was like a meeting of two minds that were seeking another part of oneselves.

Now I get to wear lots of nice frocks, jewels and tiaras and things and do a lot of important things for charity like going to balls and such like. Much more than making dollies clothes, anyway. My doll? I wouldn't leave home without it.

Irene

Paolo Martini, International Soccer Player

I was always in trouble with the referee and collected more red cards than the casino in my home town of Monte Carlo. I was born with the talent to play – clever back heels, bending long-range shots – but my concentration and discipline were incomplete. Even sometimes I would get angry with the crowds and want to kick the spectators. How could I be so stupid! I tried everything – lots of bad haircuts, silly shorts and writing a column in a tabloid newspaper – but I was never the truly great player I should have been.

Then one day a friend gave me a doll and pins and explained the ancient practice of revenge therapy. My anger left me and I became a changed player, always part of a winning team. I am now a renowned philosopher and poet, get paid huge amounts of money to advertise sports kit, have starred in two films and have a sensible haircut. I cannot thank my doll enough and always carry one in my shorts.

Ciao, Paolo

RHYMES AND RECIPES

'The doll understands the important things in life: preparing food and refreshing the spirit by writing and reciting rhymes.'

From *The Doll and the Art of Cookery and Cursing*

Rhyme Relief

Sticks and stones may break my bones, but words will break my heart', is one of revenge therapy's important tenets. Charms, spells and curses are available for every situation, but there is always room for new, improved and improvised versions. Create rhymes to meet your own particular circumstances. Making up a spell in your head is the perfect way to **keep calm in a tedious meeting**. Singing your chosen words to a popular tune adds a musical note and helps to keep the rhythm. Humming the tune out loud while singing the words in your head is particularly satisfying and can be carried out in the presence of the recipient of the spell, who will never realise what you are doing.

Ideally, your spells should be spoken at the same time as you insert pins into your doll. Advanced students will be able to project their thoughts on to the doll and simply **imagine the pins striking home**. It helps to have your doll close by, perhaps in your pocket or in a drawer of your desk.

As with all revenge therapy, spells that set up the recipient to undergo ego-deflating and embarrassing situations are the most stress relieving. The tried and tested spells below will inspire you to create your own.

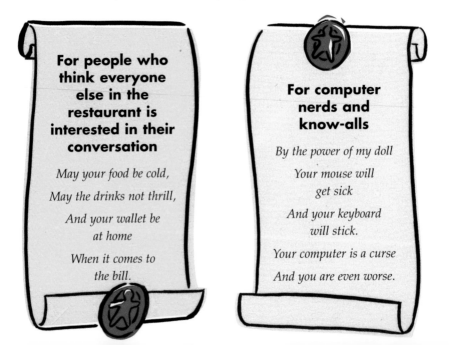

For people who think everyone else in the restaurant is interested in their conversation

May your food be cold,

May the drinks not thrill,

And your wallet be at home

When it comes to the bill.

For computer nerds and know-alls

By the power of my doll

Your mouse will get sick

And your keyboard will stick.

Your computer is a curse

And you are even worse.

For noisy neighbours

Lights fuse

Pipes burst

With this rhyme I you curse.

Noisy neighbours

Move away

Go to live in (place of your choice).

For rude people
(based on traditional African curses)

May the spot on your nose grow to the size of an elephant's ball.

Let your pig grow three ears and your dog have two noses.

Your wind will be like that of the water buffalo.

For general irritation
(traditional)

North, South, West and East,

(say recipient's name) is a beast.

East, West, North and South,

(say recipient's name) should shut his/her mouth.

Limerick-style Rhymes

The traditional limerick has the potential to fit any person or situation. Simply composing a limerick reduces stress and is a proven way of not getting mad but **getting even**. (Successful limericks can be surreptitiously circulated to other sufferers thereby spreading joy and happiness in the face of stress and suffering.) The Limerick of the Doll is given below for inspiration.

There was a doll full of power

Whose Master was feeling quite sour.

He inserted a pin

And started to grin

And his life blossomed forth like a flower.

Creative Cursing

Revenge, they say, is a dish best eaten cold and it is true that revenge therapy can be much more successful and long lasting if you take your time. Although some situations must be dealt with immediately, others can be sorted out in a longer ritual which draws the stress out of you in a very relaxing way.

The Gaelic curse given opposite is **particularly effective**. It has been passed down through 2,000 years of oral tradition and its very age makes it powerful. The secret to its success is to be relaxed during its recital. Sit in a darkened room (candlelight is ideal) and recite it slowly and clearly. Your doll is the perfect audience for your recital – hold it in your hand as you speak. Once the curse is spoken you will feel **a great sense of release**.

Many of my students find a relaxing bath is the perfect place to recite an **effective and heart-felt curse**. Privacy should be guaranteed and your doll will rest happily in the soap dish. If possible light the bathroom with red candles. As the wax melts, all the tension will drain from your body.

One note of warning – using your   pins in the bath is not recommended. It can result   in rust which will adversely affect the power   of your doll.

Gaelic Curse

The wicked who would do me harm
May he/she take the throat disease,
Spirally, virally, circularly,
Fluxy, phlegmy, swollen and grim.

Be it harder than a stone,
Be it blacker than a coal,
Be it swifter than a bird,
Be it heavier than lead.

Be it fiercer, sharper, harsher,
Than the hard, thorn-biting holly.
Be it sourer than the lemon and
the bitter salt sea.

A dysentery of blood from heart,
from mouth, from bones,
From liver, from the lobe, from the lungs,
And a scalding of veins, of throat, and
of kidneys,
To my contemners and traducers,
Seven times seven times.

In name of the doll,
Who guarded from me every evil,
And who shielded me in strength,
From the net of my breakers
And destroyers,
Seven times seven times.

The Herbal Bath

Chamomile flowers
Rosemary leaves
Dried lavender flowers

Take seven chamomile flowers and infuse them in a cupful of boiling water, leaving them to stand overnight.

Place a half-cupful of the rosemary leaves and the lavender flowers together in a small muslin bag, with a good length of string to tie the bag closed.

Hang the muslin bag under the hot tap as you run the bath so that the essential essences are flushed out. Add the chamomile infusion just before you get into the bath. In addition to helping you to relax, this bath mixture will refresh your doll, who should be positioned close by.

Kitchen Magic

Food usually has a calming effect on the mind and body and is very important in revenge therapy. You can turn a snack into a spell and reduce stress in two ways at once. You can get the day off to a good start by christening your breakfast boiled egg and **chopping off its head**. As you watch the yolk flow, imagine your stress headache floating out of your head and into the head of your oppressor. Breathe deeply. The severely stressed are recommended to draw a face on the egg before decapitating it.

A delicious extension of doll therapy is to have a bag of jellybabies on your desk or dashboard. Simply choose a baby, name it after the bastard who is grinding you down (or cutting you up in the car) and bite off its head. **Your stress levels will fall immediately.**

One of the other lecturers at Idongotu University has made a special study of the possibilities of **transferring power between a revenge doll and a jelly baby**. His research showed that 'bonding' a doll with a bag of jellybabies (simply insert the doll into the bag and leave until the moon has passed through three phases) can produce even better results.

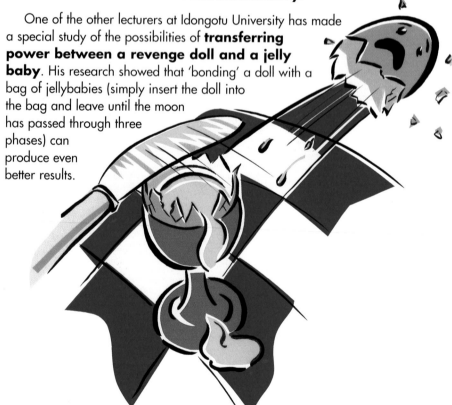

He went on to develop a very powerful therapy for treating cases of extreme tension. This involves **naming a bag of jelly babies and feeding them through a kitchen mincer**. We recommend using this technique only in very serious cases – perhaps when you feel the need to take revenge on a whole group of irritating people. Currently, this therapy is the only recorded way of dealing with the stress induced by large organisations or political parties.

Sweet Revenge

A quiet evening in the kitchen with the smells of home baking wafting around the house is guaranteed to calm you down after a stressful day. Gingerbread men and women make excellent edible voodoo dolls. This simple recipe should make about seven dolls so you can enjoy chewing over an entire army of enemies. Alternatively, take the dolls into work and give your colleagues the pleasure of biting into the boss. **Group therapy!**

You will need

225g/8oz plain flour
1 tsp ground ginger
100g/4oz butter or
  margarine
100g/4oz molasses
  sugar
100g/4oz cane
  syrup

1. Sift the flour with the ground ginger. Cream the butter or margarine with the sugar until the mixture is light and fluffy.

2. Add the flour mixture with the cane syrup and knead until smooth. Visualise the source of your stress as you knead, but try to remain calm throughout.

3. Preheat the oven to 190°C/375°F/gas 5.
Roll out the dough on a floured surface until it is approximately 3mm thick and stamp out using gingerperson cutters. Add buttons, eyes and mouths made from raisins and slivers of glacé cherries. These features will enhance the realism and, as a consequence, the stress-relieving power of the dolls.

4. Place the dolls on greased baking trays. Bake for 20 minutes. Leave to cool and name.

Making a Meal of It

While quick snacks can bring relief instantly, the advanced student might like to try an entire candlelit meal one evening, taking time to savour not just the food but the revenge as well.

A revenge meal is based on the idea of creating human forms from food, as opposed to food from human forms, or cannibalism. The skill is in the presentation and the menu can be adapted to your own or your guests' tastes. It can be as simple as egg and chips or can be a full-blown cordon bleu dinner. A few ideas to start you off are given below. When you are out shopping, keep your eyes open for any vegetables or fruits shaped like people and incorporate them into the meal.

Artichokes As you pull off each artichoke leaf, project your thoughts on to the person upsetting you and then suck hard on the leaves to weaken his or her power.

Soup with Doll Croutons Any flavour soup will do. Buy a doll-shaped cutter and cut the shapes out of bread or toast. Float them on the hot soup and watch them change colour and begin to sink before cutting them with your spoon and slurping them up.

Pastry-covered Pies Cook in the traditional way but create a face out of pastry on the crust. Visualise the face baking in the heat.

Voodoo Pizza Either make or buy the base and add the topping of your choice, designing a face or full figure as you go. Chilli, pepperoni and anything else hot are the most effective ingredients. Use a sharp knife or pizza cutter to cut up the finished result.

Ice-cream Well-frozen ice-cream can be sculpted into human form and sauces used to colour in the detail.

Fruit Salad Arrange fruit to make a figure or a face. Choosing the right colour fruit for the eyes is important. If your enemy has green eyes use kiwi fruits. For blue eyes use blueberries, red eyes raspberries and brown eyes any dried fruit such as apricots or prunes.

VOODOO FOR EVERY OCCASION

'Carry your doll on your journey through life and the road will not seem so hard nor the way so long. Your enemies will melt into the mist and unfaithful friends and lovers will find their path strewn with obstacles.'

From
The Way of the Doll

In the Office

The office is without doubt **the stress capital of life**. Irritating memos, tedious telephone calls, recalcitrant office machinery, smart-arse colleagues and bullying bosses are all part of the tension-packed picture of a working day. Openly using your doll can be difficult at times so alternative strategies may need to be employed.

Office equipment has a huge potential for crafting instant dolls. You do not have to be an origami expert to fashion dolls from paper. Cutting out with scissors is just as effective, and you can make as many rows of dolls as required. Breathe deeply, screw them up and **drop them in the waste paper basket**. If you have a shredder let the machine take the strain.

Use erasers, sticky Blu-tack and other objects to craft or mould into effigies, which can be crushed under your fist. A more sophisticated approach for the fully trained student is to **unwind paper clips and use them as pins to stick in the effigies**. A noisy, but enjoyable, remedy to office-related stress is to draw a face on a plastic or paper drinking cup and stamp on it. These can then be used as mini-frisbies to throw around the office.

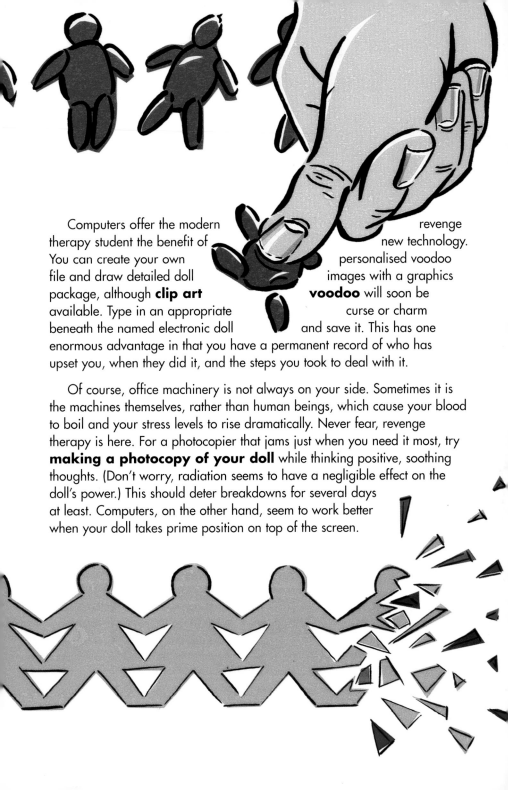

Computers offer the modern therapy student the benefit of new technology. You can create your own personalised voodoo file and draw detailed doll images with a graphics package, although **clip art voodoo** will soon be available. Type in an appropriate curse or charm beneath the named electronic doll and save it. This has one enormous advantage in that you have a permanent record of who has upset you, when they did it, and the steps you took to deal with it.

Of course, office machinery is not always on your side. Sometimes it is the machines themselves, rather than human beings, which cause your blood to boil and your stress levels to rise dramatically. Never fear, revenge therapy is here. For a photocopier that jams just when you need it most, try **making a photocopy of your doll** while thinking positive, soothing thoughts. (Don't worry, radiation seems to have a negligible effect on the doll's power.) This should deter breakdowns for several days at least. Computers, on the other hand, seem to work better when your doll takes prime position on top of the screen.

Have Doll, Will Travel

From road rage and broken-down buses to flight delays, lost luggage and cancelled trains – travelling in the late Twentieth Century has to be counted as one of our major sources of stress. It is vital, therefore, that you **always carry the doll with you** no matter how short the trip. Tuck it inside your jacket pocket for easy access or in a compartment of your travel bag.

Using pins is impractical, and potentially hazardous, in most travel situations and the recommended technique is to **squeeze the doll's neck** between your fingers and silently chant a spell, charm or curse appropriate to the situation.

A traditional 'all-purpose' travel curse has been written by one of the students who took part in the stress control experiments described at the beginning of this book. He is an airline pilot and, before taking the course, feared he would have to retire early. We are delighted to report he is back in the sky with his doll happily installed in his cockpit.

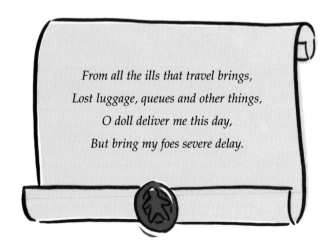

From all the ills that travel brings,
Lost luggage, queues and other things,
O doll deliver me this day,
But bring my foes severe delay.

Road Rage Cured

Of all modes of travel, it has to be driving that brings out the worst in us all. Queue-jumpers, tail-gaters, incompetent parkers and late signallers are legion. That's before we get on to roadworks and traffic wardens.

Voodoo visualisation is the key to overcoming road rage and arriving at your destination as a **calm, composed and happy human being**. Never attempt to insert pins in your doll when driving. Whenever someone cuts you up or drives too close simply visualise their exhaust pipe falling off around the next corner, or their radiator puffing hot water and steam. Rest assured, through the power of voodoo visualisation, in the morning their battery will be flat and the jump leads will have gone missing.

Some advanced revenge therapy students make special car dolls to sit on the dashboard or back shelf of the car. The presence of such a doll will help with your visualisations and will **protect you against mechanical problems and breakdowns**.

If you find yourself doll-less at any point there are other methods that can be utilised. The most popular is to write down details of the offending car's number plate and leave the piece of paper in a trash can at some forlorn location. Guaranteed misery for the owner for at least a week.

At Home With Your Doll

Home should be a haven from stress. But as we all know, nasty neighbours, revolting relatives and recalcitrant household appliances can turn haven into hell. Fortunately your doll should be particularly effective in its home environment. You will have time and opportunity to perfect your pin insertion techniques and to compose appropriate chants and curses. Moreover, there are a variety of **tension-killers ideally suited to the home environment**.

For Insomnia

General, unspecific tension and frustration sometimes needs a physical cure. A special pillow, ideally decorated with dolls, can be used as a punch bag when vengeful thoughts prevent you sleeping. **Project your hostile images on to the pillow** and try to mimic the pinning techniques from page 13 as you punch, alternating slow deliberate punches with short, sharp jabs. Using both hands dissipates the tension more quickly.

Keeping Boring People Away

Try the traditional methods of a horseshoe hung upside down above the door, planting nettles or foul-smelling assafoetida near the threshold or placing a doll stuffed with rue in the window.

Television Tantrums

Irritating TV 'personalities', particularly game-show hosts who ritually humiliate the contestants, can be dealt with by traditional doll methods. The art is to focus on the doll and **wish for some misfortune**. Will their wig slip? Will they fluff their lines? Will the participants be funnier or ruder than the host? This is something that all the family can join in and a co-ordinated effort can bring spectacular results.

Sporting events can bring great tension to the viewer. Before the game starts dress your doll in the colours of the opposition team and **keep your**

red and yellow pins handy. At critical points in the game, pin the doll in the appropriate limb. Watch the opposing team miss, fall over or lose their boots and shorts. Research has shown that all violence at sports matches can be removed if every fan is given a doll before the game.

A useful supplement to TV watching with your doll is to keep a pile of small foam rubber bricks by your side. As soon as you feel the tension rising these should be **hurled at the screen**. Some young dolls are happy to be thrown at the TV, but don't risk this unless you are sure your doll is one who does not stand on its dignity.

Annoying Neighbours

Noisy, annoying neighbours, infuriating relatives, in fact anyone who causes you undue stress and worry can be dealt with quickly and efficiently. Write their name on a piece of paper and stick it to the sole of your shoe. Walk around the house, visualising them being ground into the dirt. If you are feeling particularly **bitter or frustrated** go for a stroll around town and do your best to step in puddles, dirt, mud, or worse, depending on the degree of your irritation.

Health, Wealth and Happiness

The positive powers of your voodoo doll should not be ignored. Not only will your doll reduce stress in your life but some non-expert researchers have shown it can also cure certain ailments, stop you smoking and even make you rich.

The important thing to remember is to always use the white pin when dealing with matters of health. **Aches and pains** in any part of your body can be relieved by inserting the white-headed pin in that part of the doll's body. Leave the pin in overnight. By morning all pain should be gone.

Stopping Smoking

There are many different ways to stop smoking – hypnotherapy, acupuncture, homeopathy – but none work as well as the voodoo doll. My patented Poupette system of quitting has been used throughout the world by film stars, politicians and some of the crowned heads of Europe.

Begin each day, and end each night with the same ritual. Insert the white pin into the chest area saying slowly to yourself:

Today is it

Today I quit

No cigarette shall pass my lips

Repeat three times as you slowly insert the pin. Throughout the day **keep your doll near at hand** and every time you feel the urge for a cigarette repeat the ritual. Within 13 days all desire for nicotine will have vanished.

Gaining Wealth

There are three main ways to become wealthy – earn it, win it or marry it. Your voodoo doll can help you succeed in all three.

For winning money on the horses or any kind of numbers game use the doll as follows. Place a coin on the chest of the doll and lay out a grid of numbers or the list of runners in front of it. Take the blue pin, which signifies money, and close your eyes as you **stab the pin into the grid** or the names of the horses as you chant:

By the power of this doll
Bring me wealth and riches.
My eyes go green
And my palm itches.

For finding buried treasure, or other valuables, you will need your doll and a dowsing stick. Find a small, forked or Y-shaped branch – willow or ash is best, but any other wood will do – and hold the double ends in both hands. **Keeping the doll in your pocket all the time, walk slowly over any areas that are likely to yield treasure.** Beaches and public open spaces are ideal spots.

Lovers – Past and Present

Lovers present all kinds of problems, from desire to desire for revenge. If you need your doll to play Cupid go straight to page 44. If it is revenge you are after, read on. Revenge strategies should not be designed to harm your ex-lover, but rather to make them realise that they were **better off with you** rather than being alone, and certainly better off than being with the complete nerd/bitch they are with now. This twin approach can yield good results.

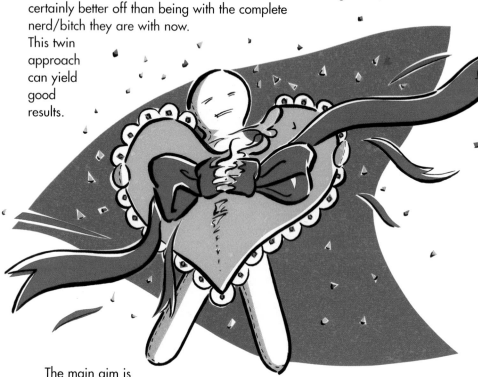

The main aim is to create a problem for your ex that only you can solve so that he or she has to see you. Obviously, your natural charm will then win them back. Losing their address book, or **a domestic crisis such as burst pipes or blown fuses can have them back with you within days.** Problems with cars are another rich source of contact.

Naturally, you will know the best way of achieving this.

A good general spell is to place a passport-sized photograph of your lost love on the face of your doll and chant:

Bring back my love (say name) who is divine
Grant this wish to make (him/her) mine
(say suitable misfortune) and make (him/her) phone
So we'll never be alone.

Another traditional doll method, without creating havoc in you lover's life, is to use the doll, with photograph attached, and place it under your pillow. Your lover will then see you in their sleep and you will be permanently on their mind. **After seven days they should be back.**

Another recommended formula is to write your lover's name on four separate pieces of paper after sunset and place them in the four corners of your house. Collect them before you go to bed and place them under your pillow. Do this with the same pieces of paper for nine days, writing the name each time. Then **burn the paper in the flame of a white candle** while you think of your lost love.

Making unfortunate things happen to your lover's new partner can bring intense satisfaction. **Large spots on their nose**, severe wind, baldness or excess body hair are all delightful misfortunes to wish upon them.

For best results insert the yellow or pink pin into the relevant segment of your doll's anatomy. (If you are feeling deeply vengeful you can use the red pin but we must issue a warning to think deeply before resorting to this.) Put the doll in a small box to concentrate its powers and, using the green pin, **attach a written description of your lover's new partner and what you would like to happen to them to the doll's chest**. Close the box and keep it shut for at least seven days. If you have a photograph of the nerd/bitch to pop in the box, so much the better.

Sit back, smile and await results.

Wedding Bells

Hoping to meet a new love, wanting someone you know to fall in love with you, or ensuring marriage all fall within the scope of stress therapy as each situation can cause deep-rooted tension and unhappiness. Some dolls are better suited to the Cupid role than others. A highly trained revenge doll may not perform at its best in a love role. If you are not getting the results you want, sew a new doll stuffed with the Love herbs listed on page 19.

To Meet a New Love

Dolls and other spells can make your one true love materialise. Pin a red paper heart (using the red pin) to your doll and place it in a window with a view of a tree – oak or ash are best. Take ten leaves from this tree and spread them around the feet of your doll. Every time you look at the doll imagine yourself in a Garden of Eden with someone you love. Their face will appear in a dream and you will meet them within seven weeks.

To Make Someone Fall For You

To attract someone you already know needs other tactics. A very elaborate ritual is to use two dolls, one to represent the partner you wish to attract, the other to represent you. Take two red candles, write the names of both parties on them, and place them on either side of the dolls. As the candles burn, imagine the two people concerned coming together and say:

Flame of passion, fire of love,

make (person's name) and (other person's name)

become hand in glove.

If it is an office romance you seek then write your name on a piece of paper and stick it under the object of your desire's chair. Be sure that your doll is in your pocket when you do this. (If you place the doll next to your heart rather than in your pocket, the strategy will be even more successful.)

Marriage

To make someone keen to marry you, pin a heart to one doll that represents your intended and another on a doll that represents you. Tie the two dolls together with red ribbon, heart to heart, and hide them among your lover's clothes for thirteen nights. Each morning remove the dolls and place them among your clothes, all the time thinking of your lover.

Testimonials

People throughout the world have written to me endorsing the power and success of the voodoo doll. Here are just a few examples.

'I used to be a boring accountant in Middlesborough, England. Since I began using the doll my life has changed considerably. I am now a boring accountant in London.'

John Jones, London

'When I was a six stone weakling, people kicked sand in my face all the time. After buying your doll and studying its methods I began to put on muscles every time I went to the gym. Now I am Mr Universe and making movies that need great big blokes all the time.'

A.S., Hollywood

'I had lots of trouble giving up smoking and drinking until I discovered the power of stress therapy. Although I still smoke cigarettes I don't inhale and if I have a beer I don't swallow it.'

B. C., Washington, DC

When I was a small girl I was very poor and dreamed of untold riches. With the help of your doll I married a very wealthy man and have wardrobes full of clothes and about two thousand pairs of shoes.'

I.M., Manila

I worked for a completely unreasonable and difficult boss for years. Then the doll gave me power to start my own business. Now I can be completely unreasonable and difficult myself!

J.S., Putney, London.

'I always wanted to have a beard so I could look like Clint Eastwood in The Good, the Bad and the Ugly but nothing would ever grow. I tried every treatment and therapy you can imagine until a friend told me about your doll. I now have stubble all over my face and do look a bit like Clint. Can you help me to grow another two foot taller?'

Watanabe San, Tokyo

'Before I practised with your doll I was so shy that I rarely went out at all except to go to work as a computer programmer. Quite frankly, I was boring. Now my life has changed and I am a liontamer in a circus and have met Barry Manilow and Gary Glitter. I certainly can recommend your doll to anyone.'

The Amazing Hilda and her Killer Lions, Paris

'I never managed to learn my times-tables at school and even had difficulty adding up. After years of study with your doll I eventually managed to solve all the problems of the universe.'

A. E., Princeton University